The Secret Life of the Little Brown Bat

Laurence Pringle

Illustrated by
Kate Garchinsky

BOYDS MILLS PRESS
AN IMPRINT OF HIGHLIGHTS
Honesdale, Pennsylvania

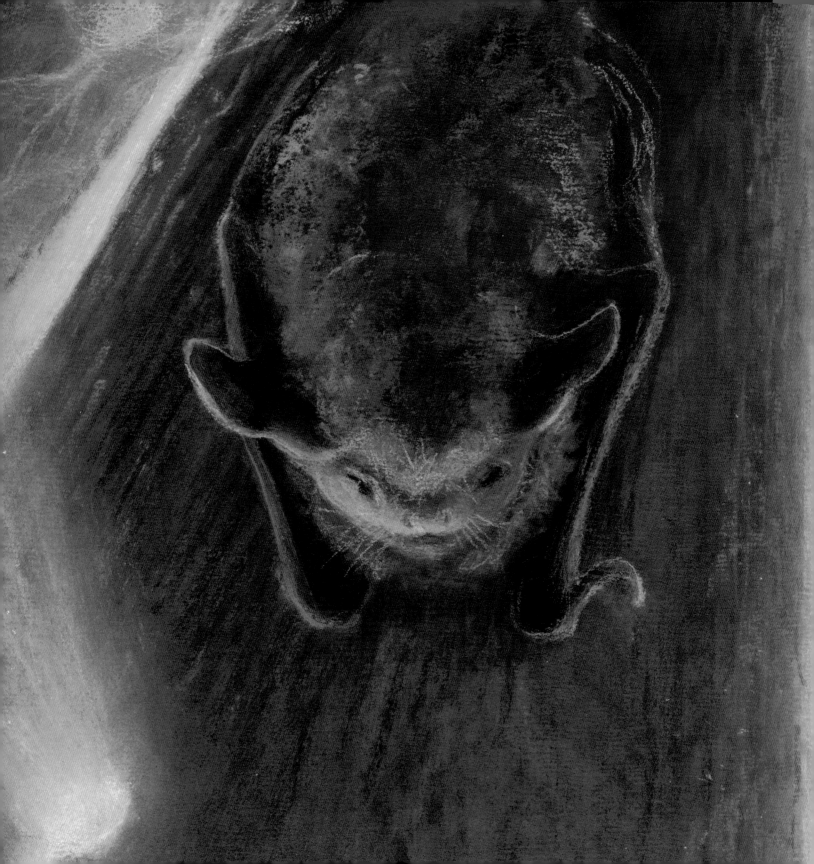

The sun has set. A July sky dims, then grows
darker. Inside the old barn, the light fades fast.
   Time to wake up! Otis yawns and stretches a wing.
His eyes wink open.

Otis hangs upside down, holding onto a wooden beam
with his toenails. He isn't quite ready to fly into the night.
First he takes time to groom. Otis uses his tongue, teeth, and
the hooked claws on his thumbs to clean his fur and wings.

Bats are Earth's only flying *mammals*, and they take very good care of their wings. Bat wings are made of thin skin that is supported by long arm bones and even longer finger bones. Otis's wings extend from his fingertips all the way back to his legs. Thin skin also stretches between his legs and tail.

Otis is a young bat. Just a few weeks ago, he was a pup, nursing milk from his mother. When Otis and his mother slept in the daytime, he snuggled under one of her wings.

They lived in a secret place—a big hollow tree—with several other mom bats and their babies, in a *nursery colony*. Young and old, they were all little brown bats, one of the most common kind, or *species*, of bat in North America.

When his mother flew out into the night to hunt for food, Otis waited. He slept close to other bat pups. Sometimes they wrestled and played, as all young mammals do.

When his mother returned, she made a squeak-chirp call. Otis answered with a whining sound. She knew him by his voice, and by the scent of his fur. She always found Otis, just as the other mothers always found their own pups.

Otis grew fast. Just three weeks after being born, he spread his wings and began to fly a little bit. Soon he was as big as his mother. He learned to catch insects to eat and no longer nursed milk.

The mothers tried their best to give their pups a good start in life. Then, in just a few nights' time, all of the moms and the young bats flew off to find new homes.

Now Otis is on his own. He hangs out with other young male little brown bats in an abandoned barn. This is their summer home, or *roost*. No one knows about their secret hideout.

After licking some dust from his wings, Otis is ready to fly. He lets go with his toe claws, spreads his wings, and flutters out of the barn. He is thirsty. He flies to a little pond. Otis swoops down, flies just above the surface, and gulps some water.

Near the pond, Otis flies higher, over a meadow. There he seems to dance in the air. With his amazingly flexible wings, Otis zigs and zags, flutters and dives, hovers and swoops, dips and swerves. Then he makes a quick turn and does it all again. And again!

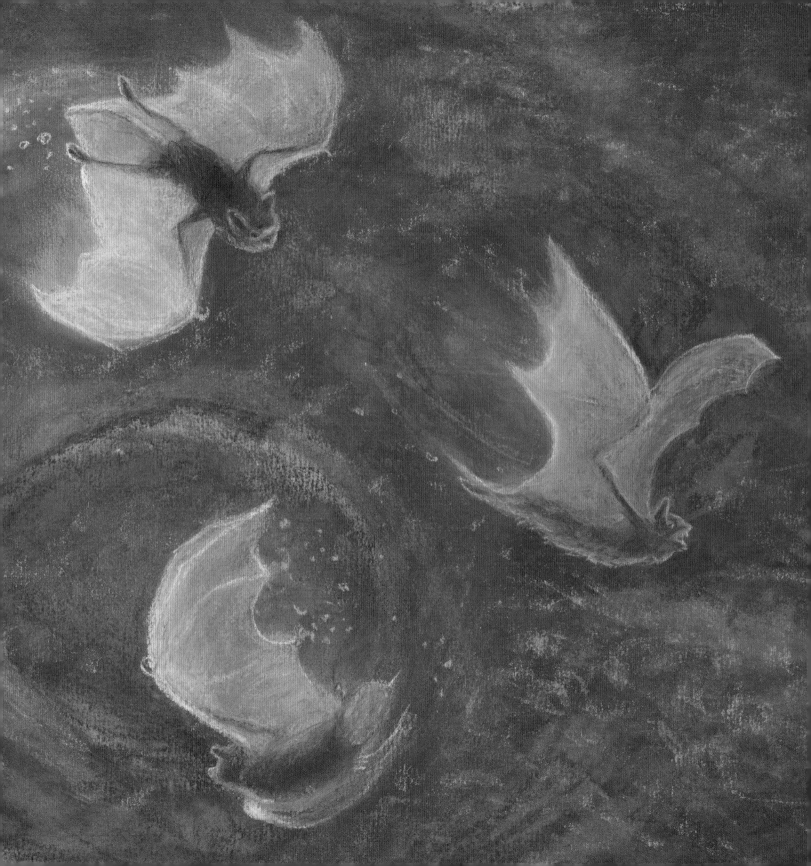

Otis is not playing. He is hunting. He is finding, chasing, catching, and eating insects. He sends out high-pitched clicking sounds that humans cannot hear (called *ultrasonic sounds*). He listens for echoes from the clicks that bounce back to his ears. From the echoes, his brain makes a picture of what lies ahead in the dark.

This is called *echolocation*. In an instant, Otis can detect a flying insect ahead. He can also tell its size, speed, and distance.

That insect is in big trouble!

As Otis flies he sends out about ten clicks a second. That changes when echoes tell him that a small moth is flying just ahead. He sends out a quick burst of ultrasounds, almost two hundred clicks a second. (This is called a *feeding*, or *terminal, buzz*.)

Otis zooms straight toward his target. He snags the
moth with one wing, then flips it into the skin between his
legs. He bends his head down, grabs the moth, chews and
swallows. This takes just a second or two. He keeps flying,
sending out more ultrasonic clicks, listening, hunting.

Otis darts, dives, turns, and twists, catching beetles, crane flies, gnats, mayflies, midges, mosquitoes, and moths. With a full belly, he flies home to his roost. He still sends out ultrasounds. Echoes that bounce back help him fly safely. He dodges wires, tree branches, or other obstacles in the air.

Inside the barn, Otis does a flying trick he has learned well. He heads straight toward a wall or ceiling, then flips in the air, turns upside down, and grabs the wood with his toenails—a perfect bat landing.

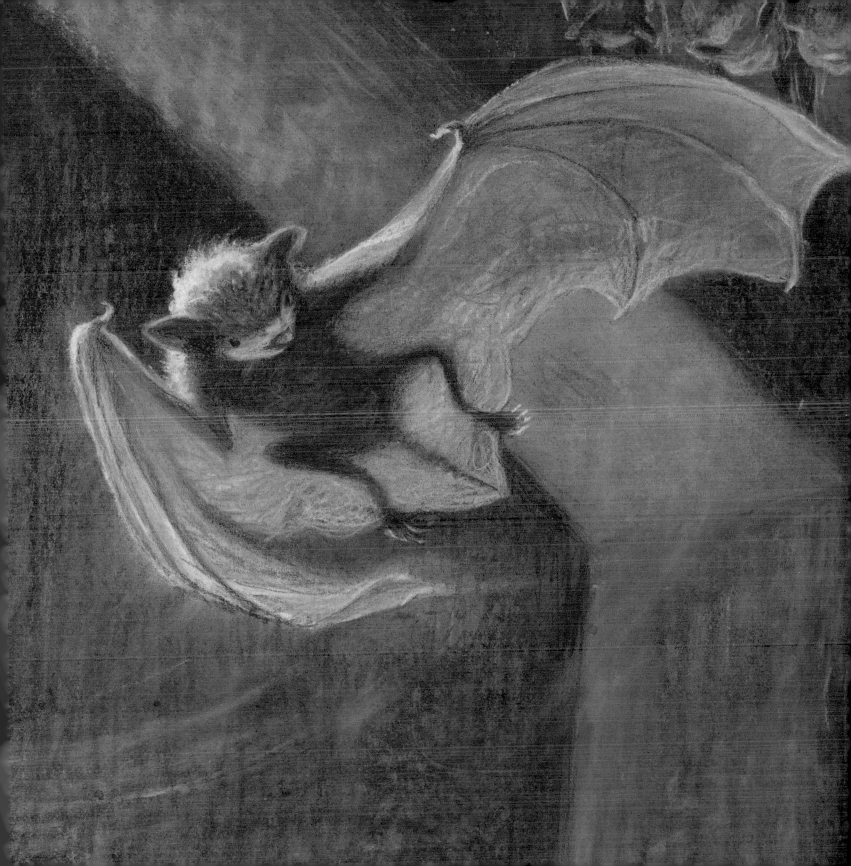

As summertime flies by, Otis learns to be a better hunter. Some nights, new kinds of flying insects appear. One evening in late August, Otis hears echoes that tell him there is a moth flying up ahead. He sends out more clicks and speeds toward it, but the moth vanishes!

It is a tiger moth, an insect that can hear ultrasounds. Tiger moths and green lacewings are two kinds of flying insects that listen for bat clicks. When they hear them, these insects may swerve, dive, or make ultrasonic clicks of their own. The moth clicks interfere with bat clicks, allowing the insects to escape.

All summer long, Otis and the other bats feel safe in their secret home, the old barn. No raccoons or other *predators* can reach the bats as they sleep high overhead. Outdoors, Otis stays alert for danger. Sometimes, echoes bounce back to him from something big but harmless—another bat, or a giant moth.

Moonlit nights can be especially dangerous for a bat that might be seen by a night-flying predator. Tonight there is a full moon.

Suddenly Otis senses something very big coming
toward him! He folds his wings and drops like a stone.
Then he flies fast and escapes from the owl.

Every night, Otis and the other bats eat a lot. They store fat
in their bodies, getting ready for winter when there will be no
insects in the air. Before that time comes, Otis and the other bats
will be in a deep, sleep-like state called *hibernation*.

On a chilly September night, Otis leaves the barn but does
not hunt. Instead, he flies fast and true for many miles.
The next day he sleeps under the loose bark of a tree,
then travels all through the night again.

At dawn he flutters into an opening in a rocky cliff, and then into a big room, deep in the rocks. This is a secret cave where little brown bats gather. Both males and females live here, and Otis meets a female who becomes his mate.

Otis and the other bats will hibernate until next spring. Then he will wake up. He will yawn, stretch, and clean his wings. Very hungry, Otis will fly out to hunt on a warm spring night.

Lots of mosquitoes and other insects will be in big trouble!

More About the Little Brown Bat

In this book, the name Otis was chosen for the bat because of the species' scientific name: *Myotis lucifugus*. In Latin, *Myotis* means "mouse-eared." *Lucifugus* means "light fleeing." Scientists often call this species little brown myotis because there are a dozen other species of mouse-eared bats in North America and about one hundred worldwide.

Bats are the only mammals that fly. Those called flying squirrels simply glide, while bats are skilled aerial acrobats with powered flight. Both inside and outside their bodies, bats are well-adapted for flight. For example, in one night a little brown bat may eat insects that add up to half its own weight. A nursing mother eats even more, sometimes as much as her whole body weighs. What a load to carry! However, bats digest food very quickly. Just twenty minutes after eating they may start getting rid of waste—and weight—from their bodies.

Bats have lightweight bones, small bodies, and big wings. A little brown bat, for example, weighs only about two and a half ounces (about as much as a chicken egg). Its body is mouse-sized, but its wings span nine to eleven inches. (Fruit bats of Asia, Africa, and Australia may have wings up to six feet across!) Big or small, bat wings are amazingly flexible, and quite different from bird wings. The scientific name of all bats, *Chiroptera*, gives a clue about these special wings. It means "hand wing." The long, slender fingers of a bat's hand reach far from its body. A bat can move its thumbs and fingers in different ways, just as humans can flex their thumbs and fingers. This enables a flying bat to quickly change its wing shape, and also its speed and direction.

Bats are remarkable animals in other ways too. For example, they can live for many years. This is unusual—small animals tend to live short lives. Most mice and other rodents often live one year or less. One little brown bat lived in the wild for thirty-three years!

The large size of bat pups is also remarkable. They are born very well-developed. This helps them to quickly reach adult size and become independent. A little brown bat pup weighs about one quarter of its mother's weight. In humans, this would be like a 120-pound woman giving birth to a 30-pound infant!

The lives of bats are still full of mysteries. We know that bats have good vision. ("Blind as a bat" is nonsense.) A bat setting out to hunt in the evening probably sees trees and other details as well as rodents or rabbits. But what kinds of images does echolocation create? Since a little brown bat can catch tiny mosquitoes in the dark, we know that echoes give it clear details. What a bat actually sees in its brain may never be known.

What is definitely known about bats is that they are intelligent, gentle, and among the most beneficial animals on Earth. All over the world, bats do tremendous good in nature. Some species pollinate flowers of vital plants. Others spread tree seeds in tropical forests. Bats prey on insects, including some that are pests of garden plants and agricultural crops.

Little brown bats and some other small *Myotis* species also eat mosquitoes. There are claims that one little brown bat can eat hundreds of mosquitoes in one hour. That is only true if a hungry bat is let go inside an enclosed space with a huge number of mosquitoes. A little brown bat hunting at night would not normally find that many. Nevertheless, they do eat some, and they help people because mosquitoes can be annoying pests and sometimes spread diseases.

Bats themselves may carry a dangerous disease called rabies. In a huge bat colony, only a few bats might have rabies. They soon die. To be safe, never touch a bat, even one found dead. You don't have to be close to bats to appreciate and admire them.

A Terrible Disease Threat to Bats

Little brown bats are the most widespread species in North America. They were once one of the most plentiful bat species of North America. That is no longer true because they, and other bat species, are being killed by a disease, caused by a fungus, called white-nose syndrome (WNS).

In ten years, this disease has caused the death of more than six million hibernating bats in more than twenty states and five Canadian provinces. That includes about 90 percent of little brown bats in eastern North America. The disease affects some species more than others, and little brown bats are among the most heavily affected. Bats reproduce slowly. For example, little brown bat females usually have just one pup a year. It will take many years for their populations to recover.

Glossary

Echolocation: in bats, an ability to locate and catch prey, and also fly safely, avoiding obstacles in the air, by sending out sounds and listening to and interpreting the returning echoes

Feeding, *or* terminal, buzz: a rapid burst of ultrasonic clicks emitted by a bat as it closes in on insect prey. At this moment a bat may send out as many as two hundred clicks in one second.

Hibernation: in bats, a sleep-like state used to conserve body fat and energy, which may last as long as five to eight months of fall, winter, and early spring. The body temperature of a hibernating bat drops to near the air temperature in the cave. The bat seems barely alive and may breathe just twice in an hour.

Mammals: warm-blooded animals with hair or fur that give birth to live young. Female mammals can feed their young with milk from mammary glands. Bats, dogs, cows, and humans are all mammals.

Nursery colony: a group of female bats, gathered in a very warm and dark place to give birth to young (called pups) and care for them

Predators: animals that kill and eat other animals for food. Many kinds of bats are predators, though some species eat fruit, pollen, or nectar. Some bat species have unusual prey: fish, frogs, birds, or other bats. The food of three species of vampire bats is blood from mammals or birds.

Roost: a place used for rest or sleep by some kinds of animals, including birds and bats. Caves, attics of houses, and abandoned mines can be used as roosts for bats. Some bat roosts can give shelter to many thousands of bats.

Species: organisms, such as plants or animals, that have characteristics that differ enough from other organisms that they do not interbreed. For example, little brown bats do not mate with California bats, northern long-eared bats, or other bat species.

Ultrasonic sounds: sounds that are "high-pitched," beyond the range of human hearing. Many species of bats use ultrasonic sounds to navigate and find prey in the dark.
See **Echolocation.**

Dedicated to Andrew Gutelle and Sena Messer, good writers and good friends, met long ago under Chautauqua's bat-dappled sky. —LP

For my new godchild and nephew, Gavin. While I learned how to draw bats for this book, you learned to smile. That grin is all over these pages. Keep smiling and learning to love, and I will too. —KG

The author and illustrator thank Aryn P. Wilder, PhD, Department of Natural Resources, Cornell University, for her careful review of the text and illustrations.

The illustrator thanks Stephanie Stronsick, Founder and Director of Pennsylvania Bat Rescue, for providing a closer look at live bats, and for returning hundreds of rehabilitated bats to the skies each year. facebook.com/pabatrescue

🔖 BOYDS MILLS PRESS
An Imprint of Highlights
815 Church Street
Honesdale, Pennsylvania 18431
boydsmillspress.com
Printed in China

ISBN: 978-1-62979-601-7
Library of Congress Control Number: 2017949842
First edition
10 9 8 7 6 5 4 3 2 1

The text of this book is set in Mercurious CT Light.
The illustrations are done in pastels and aqua crayons on sanded paper.

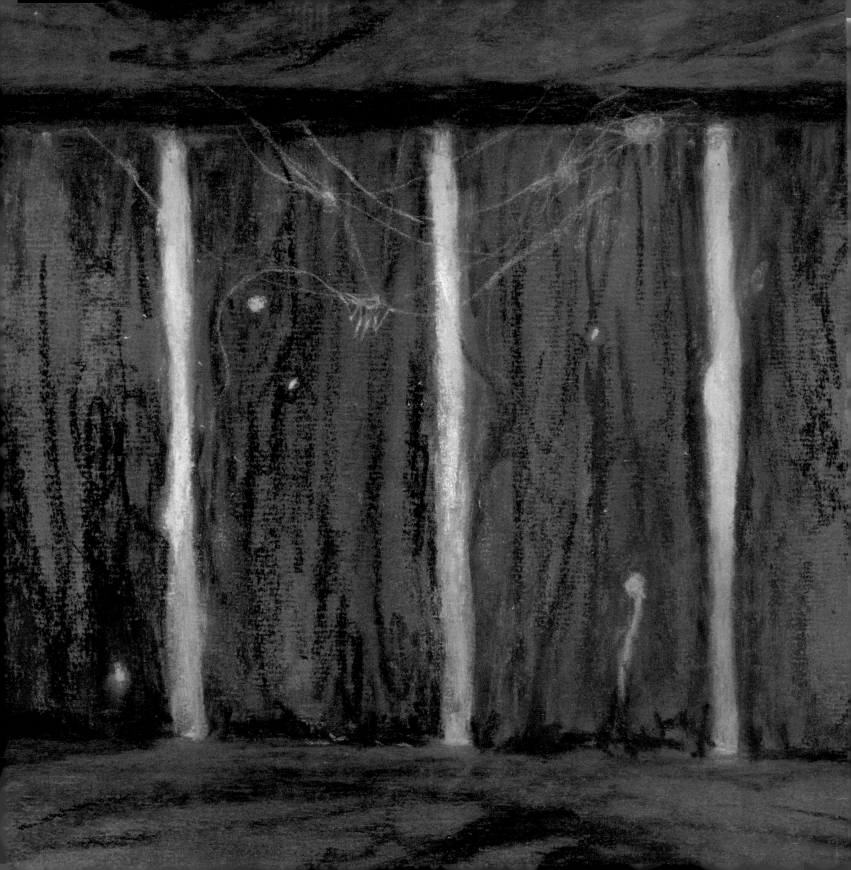